No Chicken in Our Pot

S. Lee Schauer

Published by Spearmint Books

Copyright © 2014 S. Lee Schauer
All rights reserved.

This book or any portion thereof may not be reproduced or used in any manner whatsoever without the express written permission of the publisher, except for use of brief quotations as in a book review.

Published by Spearmint Books, Vacaville, CA
Printed in the United States of America.

First Printing, 2014

978-09884631-2-7

Acknowledgements

First, to all my children, whose memories
of these times are not only more clear, but different.

Thanks to my good friends for their
continuing encouragement.

Special thanks to:
Betty Lucke, who helped put it all together

Deni Harding, The Champion of the Apostrophe,
for her editing help

and to all of the
Town Square Library Writing Group

Dedicated to

Terri, Douglas, Chuck and David,

Brave Adventurers All

Table of Contents

Preface 11

No Chicken in Our Pot 1

Country Dreaming 2

Welcome to Eden 4

Grab the Scrub Brush 6

Spirit Watch 8

Let's Get Moving 12

All Wet 14

Whee ! 16

Danger ! 17

Antique Treasure Trove 19

Not Tarzan 20

Heavenly 21

Ghost ? 23

Soft Furry Fun 25

Get the Jackets 26

A Happy Blaze 28

Our Own Road	30
Small Town Business	33
Settling In	35
Snow Here?	38
Living Country	39
Spanish Interlude	40
Chickens, Chickens, Chickens	41
Chopping Block	43
Roosters	45
Buckwheat	47
Pony Ride	49
Budding	53
Solitude	55
Gardening	57
Oh, Nuts	59
Fruits of Our Labor	61
Outside Business	63
Ol' Water Hole	64
Drink of Life	66
Ducks Galore	67
Goosed	68
Sheba	71
Enter the Boys	75

Crossing the Line	78
What's That Smell?	80
More Soft and Fuzzy	82
Henry and Bear	84
You'll Shoot your Eye Out	86
Who Was It ?	88
Poor Bird	89
Green Eggs and Ham	91
Kick the Bucket	93
Released	95
Burial Grounds	96
Integration	97
Bad Rooster	99
Giddi-up	101
Sorry, Terri	102
Cattle Auction	104
Bandit	105
Just Like Kittens	108
Lucky Truck ?	110
Sweetie Face	112
Adventurers	116
All Wet	118
Archie Bread	120

Dive in the Hive	122
Not Lit Up	123
A Break in the Wood Shed	125
Sam	127
Look Out, Mouse	128
That's Scary	129
Shocking	131
Sadness	133
Snakes	134
A Wolf ?	136
Doggie Problems	137
Changing with Time	139
Memories Remain	142
About the Author	146

Preface

One of my fondest memories is of a country road in rural Tennessee. That two-lane road dipped and curved through fields, past farm houses and had dogs running out to it to greet visitors.

I was around eight years old and we were visiting relatives who had a sprawling home there. They must have just kept adding on to the main house as more children arrived. Then they turned their garage into a small country store. There were children, dogs, cats, chickens and the ever-present aroma of biscuits cooking. I watched in wonder as huge meals were served three times a day, to large numbers of people. So different from the way I lived as an only child in a city in California!

There was a large hen house in the back, with clucking chickens that laid real brown eggs. I was allowed to collect the eggs every morning. They marveled that a city girl was not afraid to lift up a big hen and snatch that egg out of the nest. I loved it!

The first sight I saw each morning when I looked up from the sofa where I slept, was of two horses on the hill across the road. One morning the horses were gone and a blanket of snow covered the hillside. Wow! I ran out in my bare feet to feel and taste it! There were even foot-long icicles hanging from the roof! Never had I experienced wonders such as this.

I never forgot that warm, welcoming farm, or those chickens. For a short time I had a chance to try to reproduce those scenes, minus the snow, of course. Kids, dogs, cats, chickens, laughter, and the aroma of baking bread.

Author's Note

The photos are precious memories of a long-ago time. They may lack in sharp photographic excellence, but they capture the joy and the love of those years. They are what they are.

No Chicken in Our Pot

Why would anyone rush off to live far away from other people, out in the country, very near the scene of a grisly murder? That's what I had been asking myself, and now here we were driving down a two-lane country road. The driveway at the new place was only a few feet from where the Zodiac killed his first victims just three years ago! He had begun his career as a notorious serial killer when he killed those two kids parked on the roadside, shot them on their first date. Lake Herman Road: the name itself had become synonymous with the Zodiac. He had bragged about the murders, using the sign of the zodiac in his letters to newspapers as his calling card. He went on to have five confirmed victims and maybe several more by this time. He was probably long gone by now, maybe in prison on another charge, and it had all happened three long years ago. I really worked hard to justify moving out there.

Country Dreaming

Oh, what a dream come true—to live in the country. A big plus was better schools for Dave, almost six, who bravely tromped forward to keep up with his brothers, eight-year-old Chuck, sweet and gentle, who would love to have a kitten, and ten-year-old Douglas, the tough guy who met every challenge and conquered. Terri, at fourteen, would start a much safer high school and was more interested in her friends and clothes than country life even she had to admit it was beautiful.

Unforeseen circumstances had caused us to move from the home we loved and had been in for years. What with summer and YMCA day camp just starting, there was no time to really look for anything suitable, so we rented a place in Vallejo which none of us liked. I was the assistant camp counselor and Terri a junior counselor, and the boys went along as campers. We were rarely at home, spending every day swimming, crafting, and various sports—with a one-night sleep over each week in the hills around Lake Chabot. Now that was behind us, summer was over, camp ended, and a new life just starting for us all.

We would all experience the country, small town living, and new adventures. Yes, but, I reasoned with myself, the Zodiac killed his next victim on the Fourth of July just three miles away at Blue Rock Springs, a park we often visited and I would be alone with the four kids most of the time. Right, I countered, but now we can have a dog or cat or whatever we wanted. The last thought won and I shut off the rest as we turned onto the old road that ran beside Blue Rock Springs, curved past pastures with real cows grazing, an occasional farm house and a picture-perfect lake.

Here it is - Home, Sweet Home

Welcome to Eden

On the left side at the bottom of a downward curve there was the mail box tilting on an old post; it stood as described without a number on it. There appeared to be no addresses out here; we merely followed the given directions. The house couldn't be seen from the road—just trees and hills. There was a large gate, over a grate that cattle hesitated to cross, that must be opened and shut each time someone drove through. That job that went to Dave, who being the youngest didn't yet know to complain. We drove around a bend, over a small stream crossed by a cattle grate bridge that dipped down and threatened to cave in as we crossed it, and there we were. What was left of an old barn sagged on the left while a better old barn stood further on. Several old wooden buildings stood in various states of disrepair, tucked between huge eucalyptus trees, lined the road leading up to the main building. There was even an old hand water pump near the last out-building. The whole place almost had the appearance of a little old ghost town.

 The house stood quietly at the end of the road. It had been built over sixty-eight years before, and whatever color it used to be had faded long ago. The house now blended softly into the fields and hills surrounding it. A wraparound porch on two sides led from the living room door around to the back bedroom. The soft rolling hills had just finished being baked all summer and glowed like gold in the lowering sun. Dark rocks dotting the hillsides made me think of chocolate chips in cookie dough, one of my favorite things. If we had inherited a palace, we couldn't have been more thrilled. It just needed a little love and fixing up.

Grab the Scrub Brush

The screen porch facing the driveway was unlocked, so the kids and I entered a cluttered, enclosed porch, kicked trash out of our way, and peered through the glass kitchen door.

"Wow," Douglas exclaimed, squinting for a better look. "Look at all those mice!"

Mice were running over the top of an old stove and in and out of the burners. It looked like a mouse party.

"Well, we will get a cat," I reassured them.

What a lovely antique of a stove—cream-colored with green trim and the word "Malleable" written in script on the front. It even had shelves built into the back that turned out to be places to set bread to rise. It just needed lots of cleaning.

Chuck and David took turns looking, too, and then explored the remains of various bags, rags, scraps of wood, bits of bones, (*I hope they had a dog,*) and other potential treasures left behind on the porch. Lots of cleaning needed!

Spirit Watch

It had been standing empty for over a year, so after we got the key we went walking through *feeling it.* The kids believed I had the power to detect ghosts or bad *feels,* and maybe I believed it too. The main living area felt wonderful. Four large bedrooms, a large living room, and a small family room with a real fireplace. Best of all, a large country kitchen with that huge stove that had a place next to the burners where you could stuff paper and small pieces of wood to burn to keep everything warm and cozy. I found this to be very useful later on, warming the kitchen on cold mornings. Every room had windows providing us with views of hills and trees all around. No other homes or roads could be seen. We soon realized the room I called a bedroom at the back of the house used to be a parlor, and the hallway door leading from it had been the front entrance. Stairs led off the porch down to what had been a paved walkway. "Marshall 1903" was engraved on one of the paver stones. The yard was all overgrown with weeds; if there had ever been a drive way, it had been obscured long ago.

The old house must have been grand in its day. I pictured guests seated in the parlor while coffee and pastries were readied in the kitchen. A small pantry hid the sink and work area, and an opening, a kind of silent butler, connected to the kitchen to pass things through—very handy while clearing the table. Next to it was a small door that opened to allow an ironing board to extend. Will wonders never cease? When did modern living force us to give up these luxuries?

There were a few challenges, too: the pipe under the kitchen sink was broken off and led directly to a bucket that would need to be emptied several times during dish washing. Well, things were certainly easier than in the old days when water also had to be pumped in, and I felt good conserving water by watering the plants with the dish water. This feeling wasn't always present later after carrying several buckets a day!

Then there was the cellar. A door from the kitchen led down a flight of steep stairs to the darkness below. We had magic protection so down the Alfred Hitchcock stairs we went with sage and matches to smudge all uneasy feelings away. It was a dark descent since the light switch was a funny-looking button located at the bottom of the stairs. The basement had obviously been converted to an apartment long before and had been in the process of converting back for many years. All that remained now was sludge from broken pipes on the floor, ragged curtains on the windows, and spiders fleeing from the light as we approached. Even so, it felt fine. This is where Christmas decorations and tons of other boxes from years of accumulation would be stored. Later we would discover our rubber Santa holding a small Coke bottle had gotten his fingers chewed off by something the size of a rat. Either there weren't many rats or they hid from us, as not one was ever seen.

One small room in the corner of the basement was behind a closed door, and once we entered, we saw it had no windows. It was under the kitchen area and was unnervingly dark. There were the remains of several wooden boxes with what might have been meat packed in salt long ago. I couldn't say what that fatty, gristly material had been, and I didn't care to delve into it further. I did know that in the days before refrigeration, meat was packed in salt and kept in a cool place to avoid spoilage. Probably that was the case here. Nevertheless, it gave me the shivers. I smiled and declared it interesting so as not to frighten the kids, but they could feel it too. This was a bad, scary place with a heavy, omnipresent feeling pressing down on us. We quickly left and shut the door behind us. I don't think anybody ever entered it again while we were there. We kept the door at the top of the stairs locked most of the time, too, thus we remained safe and cheerful.

.

Let's Get Moving

The very next night we started the task of moving in our small, breakable things. Terri and I went first in the car with vases, pictures, and what not, all the while discussing the Zodiac murder and other things gory that might happen on a quiet, dark country road. Then we noticed a vehicle getting closer behind us. It was dusk, and I began to be afraid to stop and open the gate with someone so close behind.

"Hold on!" I shouted. "I am going to head for town," and stepped on the gas. What a scary feeling! The headlights came even closer and then blinked, and a horn honked loudly. I looked back and realized it was my husband, Doug, who was also bringing a carload of stuff. He was away from home quite a bit due to work and other issues, had not been a part of the moving process before, so I had just forgotten he was there this time.

"What were you doing?" he yelled rudely after I pulled over.

"Just being silly," I answered and looked at him like he should have known that.

Terri wisely didn't say anything. We soon became accustomed to driving and sometimes walking on that road and never worried about it again.

Douglas and Bear by creek

All Wet

The first day in the new house was warm and the three boys yelled, "We want to go skinny dipping in the creek like country people!" It was a shallow, private creek, so I thought, why not? That is what country people did, didn't they? I didn't have long to debate the idea. Ten minutes later three wet, muddy, subdued boys were back.

"There's snakes in there," Douglas informed me.

"Yeah," echoed David.

Chuck had a pinpoint red dot on his forehead. "I slipped on the muddy bank getting out and hit my head on a piece of barbed wire," announced Chuck. If there was a way to get hurt, he would find it.

So much for skinny dipping.

Whee !

They soon discovered another way to have fun—using a large plastic boat as a sled to slide down the steep, grass-covered hill behind the house. They had their very own slide. This provided them with hours of fun each day until the boat cracked and fell apart.

Then they used their round metal saucers meant for the snow. Once those were ruined, they resorted to plastic bags or anything they could find for sliding. A little bumpy at times but no one got hurt.

Danger !

David soon found a great toy. Our road forked off at an old barn that had the remains of a fire truck next to it, growing out of the weeds. Its bright red had faded to a light rust color and the tires were almost disintegrated. Research revealed it to be a 1932 Ford fire truck, topless for easy access, whose hood opened from each side. The back was filled with branches and old debris. The fun of opening and closing the hood and crawling all over that fire truck would not have been allowed had I known, so I am glad I didn't.

I do wish I had been aware of other things that David played with, though. It was not until many years later he advised me of the barrel he had discovered in the back of an unused shed with a powdery substance that he ran his hands through and tossed up in the air to watch it float and sparkle. He and Chuck coated their arms with the silvery, glittery stuff and pretended to be superheroes flinging their arms about. I was blissfully unaware that our lake was tainted with mercury; I had no idea the surrounding hills had been mined for the stuff. The writing on the front of the barrel said **"Mercury"**, but I never saw it.

Antique Treasure Trove

This was a wonderful place for exploring, an activity they never seemed to tire of. The boys dug up a pile of old bottles, some cobalt blue like Vicks and Milk of Magnesia, some with rotted cork in the top. We decided that long ago the trash that couldn't be burned was buried for us to discover later. There was an old water pump still in the ground by the side of the house, and old harnesses and farm equipment rested in some of the sheds. There were barrels of other unknown powder (more mercury?) and boxes of unidentifiable stuff. What kind of people lived here in the far past? What did they do? I wish we had more clues.

Not Tarzan

There was a giant eucalyptus tree in the back yard close to the house. The previous tenants had built large plywood platforms in its branches and attached one to another with ropes and pulleys. It looked like something out of Robinson Crusoe or Tarzan. What fun for children to play in!

"Don't let them near it," flatly stated their dad.

I was more disappointed than they were. I would have loved it when I was a kid! I wanted to show him it was safe and called him out to see Chuck demonstrate how easy and fun it could be. (Whatever made me choose Chuck?) I think Chuck might have been on the lowest platform two minutes before he fell to the ground with a terrible thud. He was, thankfully, unharmed, and we left the tree alone without further argument.

Douglas with baby fox

Heavenly

What an enchanted land to live in at night! No street lights or other houses around, so we were afforded a glimpse of the night sky not viewed in town. All those stars! The boys had a telescope; while not the most accurate, it was certainly fun. Chuck tells of a time he climbed onto the roof for a better view—another adventure I was unaware of. Once while watching the stars in the evening, we saw a star moving forward, then quickly zip back in the opposite direction and was gone! Yes, the kids and I really believe we saw a UFO.

The air smelled like eucalyptus and a good earthy aroma, like baked wheat, at night in the summer when the heat cooled down. Groups of eucalyptus trees, with their branches so high and thick it was impossible to see up into them, supported an owl or two. They were rarely seen but certainly heard in every tree every night. The barn had an owl high up in the rafters.

We also heard a chorus of yips like puppies and guessed they were baby foxes as we often saw a red or grey fox run across the road or in the distance. Soon after we moved in, Douglas found a baby fox and of course carried it home to show us. It was very calm and docile, like a puppy. I hope it found its way back to its family when he returned it from where it was found.

Ghost ?

I suppose this is where I will mention the party—although it's not in the category of wild life. It was certainly a new phenomenon that I had not experienced before coming to the farm.

One of the first nights, as I was in bed with my head on the pillow, I heard something. At first I was afraid it might be something by the bed—a mouse? No, nothing there. Once settled on the pillow again, I realized the sounds seemed to arise from the basement below. The murmuring of a crowd; faint laughter, mostly female? The occasional clinking of glasses? Yes, there was a party in the basement!

This continued most every night during the time we lived there, and I came to feel it was just a harmless part of the atmosphere. I only noticed it when my head was on the pillow. I now wonder why I hadn't asked the kids if they were aware of these sounds. I suppose I felt the less said the better.

Years later I met someone who had also lived there and heard the same party! No, I did not go downstairs to investigate—not at night.

Soft Furry Fun

The ad said, "Beautiful, free kittens!" And they were beautiful: calico and tortoise shell with black, white and orange long hair. Just what I had always wanted.

"Look how cute they are together. A shame to separate them," the lady told me. They tumbled together on the carpet and were beautiful. I hesitated taking two females and then remembered there were no other houses for miles, thus no other cats. I had a lot to learn about animals—which I proceeded to do the hard way.

Get the Jackets

I heard the large truck before it made the last turn into the driveway. It was the propane man. I wondered what he wanted. I had signed up for electricity in town and assumed that it included gas, as it always had. Wrong again.

"I'm here to fill your tank, and I won't make another stop here till spring. This road gets impassable when it rains," he told me with a flat look.

It does? I was not aware of that important fact. The heater and stove were both gas.

"What does it cost?" I asked while trying to keep the anxiety out of my voice.

"About $100.00, and you need to sign up for service in Napa."

I felt a quick panic; a hundred dollars was a lot of money, but I decided to follow his advice, digging the money out of the emergency fund and planning a fast trip to Napa.

The living room heater had a thermostat and kept us nice and warm for about one month until it ran out of propane. It was a big stand-up heater that the boys would rush to get dressed in front of on cold winter mornings. It took them longer than it should to learn that when you bend over to pull up your pants, your back side hits the heater. All three boys had four little burn scars, like tines on a fork where no one would see them. Thankfully I was able to talk the propane man into another visit, paid another one hundred dollars and turned the heater off. I learned to be a heat-and-propane miser.

So much to learn, and the lessons kept on coming.

Jousting for warm cozy spots

A Happy Blaze

We learned cause-and-effect truths that townies couldn't know. We knew the joy of working together tearing down that old barn for the wood, sawing and chopping tree limbs, and crowding around the fireplace to enjoy the fruits of our labor. The dog usually scored the best place in front of the fire and was almost impossible to move. The cats curled up on top of whomever had found a warm spot lying by the fire.

We also obtained the sad knowledge that freshly-cut trees don't burn, especially the hard eucalyptus that we spent so many hours chopping and sawing. Even Dave and Chuck, the two youngest, did their part—lugging bags and laundry baskets full of scrap wood every day in the winter. After we lit the first roaring fire, I happened out back to pick up more wood, and suddenly flames on the roof caught my eye. The roof was blazing merrily, too! I was so shocked it took a minute before I grabbed the hose and put it out. Then we had to take a ladder to peer into the attic rafters to make sure a spark hadn't worked its way in. I was not aware chimneys usually had some sort of screen over them, and even if I had known, I doubt I could have reached it. This unplanned blaze happened frequently when papers or anything other than wood was burned. It became routine to watch for fire on the roof.

Road fixing - a never-ending job

Our Own Road

It was about a quarter of a mile from the house down a dirt road that had some gravel and gunnite added to it. Then we would reach the two-lane road where the school bus barreled around the corner to pick up the kids each morning. I heard the rock-and-roll music blaring over the hillside before I saw the bus. Propane man was right: the road fell in on itself and turned to mud after the rains began. The gunnite that made a fine grit that blew in the air when dry didn't help at all when wet. The kids' father, Big

Doug, had brought gunnite home from his workplace and spread it on the road in a futile attempt to change the dirt to a harder material .The kids kept their school shoes in the mail box and sloshed back and forth in rubber boots. The mailman never ventured out this far. I wondered if he ever had. Why was a mail box here?

Walking on this road often presented other problems in the form of cows. They were beef cattle owned by the landlord, and they grazed in the fields all around with nothing stopping them from walking on the roads. Luckily I had joined the kids for our first encounter with them. The road was around twelve feet wide with a hill on one side and a creek on the other. It became common place while walking the road to come upon a group of cows.

Since beef cattle weigh around fifteen hundred pounds apiece they could appear threatening, and we were not used to animals that just stood their ground and stared with eyes as big as saucers. They let us come up as close to them as six feet, then they would act startled, jump in the air, and turn and run a few feet down the road. It was quite unnerving at first.

I do think of all the meat people consume, cows are best suited for the job. They strike me as very stupid creatures. If we didn't yell and chase them when they first turned to run, they would stop just a few feet down the road, and we would have to repeat the scene again. We often saw fox, quail, pheasant, and other small animals that were wise enough to run at first glance.

Small Town Business

I now had to have my mail delivered to a post-office box. The post office was an old converted Victorian house. How nice to park right in front and never stand in line. The only time there was a wait was when the post-master was catching up on the news of the day with another patron, and I enjoyed listening in. Once I mistakenly left my wallet in a phone booth in town and despaired of ever seeing it again. The post-master called; someone found it and turned it in to the post-office. The few dollars were still in it.

The library was also an old converted Victorian with a cozy fireplace. This was one of my favorite places to relax and take a break. The librarian behind the desk was always smiling and ready to recommend something new and delightful to read.

On a few occasions, before it finally closed its doors, the kids and I went to the old movie theater downtown. It sold popcorn and candy and had one viewing room with one screen. On at least two visits, we were the only customers there. I knew it could not last long at that rate even though it was the only theater in town.

We had a small town newspaper that was delivered once a week. Of course it did not come out as far as our farm; it had to be picked up in town.

Me, Douglas and Chuck

Settling In

I turned country music on the radio. We watched *The Waltons*, *Little House on the Prairie*, and, of course, *Bonanza* on our black and white TV that sported aluminum-foil-wrapped rabbit ears. I bought us all overalls and straw hats and browsed the library for stories of first-timers new to country living and laughed at some of the mistakes they made.

At night Terri would start the routine, a parody of "*The Waltons*", by calling out "Good night, Doug boy!"

followed by silence. "Goodnight, Chuck boy! Goodnight David boy!"

They in turn answered, "Goodnight, Terri"

Then she would repeat the phrase again to Douglas who finally would reply in a gruff voice, "Goodnight, Terri!"

There were several old outbuildings to explore and a half- collapsed barn. The small building closest to the house with the best roof was soon turned into the woodshed. Another small building had only a few shingles missing and even had electricity. I found a box of composite shingles, got out a ladder, and patched the few places where the roof might leak. The other roofs were way beyond my capability.

Terri fixed that small building so it looked quite cozy to invite her friends for a sleepover. Chuck would take his portable record player and play his favorite Ricky Nelson and Elvis forty-fives.

A good sized building placed somewhat between the house and the barn appeared round or almost octagon-shaped. We were told by an older person who knew some of the history that the round house was the first structure built on this land and had been intended to be the start of a house for the builder's new bride. When she ran off before the wedding, he left everything and sold the land. This must have taken place around the turn of the twentieth century. Kind of made me sad thinking of broken dreams. Now it was a storehouse for dust-laden junk.

Snow on the water pump

Snow Here?

It even snowed the first year we were there! We ran outside with our hands in the air to catch precious snowflakes. It made a white dotted veil between us and the tall hills enclosing us. We had never seen snow where we lived before! It melted in hours, though, and really added to our country experience. Going to a school play that night, we saw the parked cars covered with a fine coating of snow while the school kids inside sang their rehearsed song with the words, "It never snows in Benicia."

Living Country

In the evening the kids and I would sit in a semi-circle on the carpet while I read chapters from *Little Britches* by Ralph Moody. The beginning stories started with "Father and I were Ranchers" and told of his childhood days on a farm in Colorado and the hardships they endured. The kids loved it. Soon Douglas went around wearing his straw hat, a piece of straw hanging from the corner of his mouth making country remarks such as, "What fer?"and "Howdy" and "I reckon".

.

Chuck leading, Dave riding

Spanish Interlude

I heard him well before he appeared over the hill, his beautiful voice singing in Spanish with such feeling, echoing over the hills. I didn't need to speak Spanish to know his songs were about love and the joy of life. He looked noble, beautiful, and proud riding a huge black horse. I tried talking to him with my few words of Espanol, but I had to give up. I assumed he herded or somehow accounted for the cattle that grazed on these acres. I had the pleasure of hearing him several times a year.

Famous chicken yard

Chickens, Chickens, Chickens

The remains of an old chicken yard made me wonder what raising chickens would be like. Now I know why that stuff was called "chicken wire", and I started replacing a good-sized chicken yard with tons of it. It is not that easy to cut apart, but I persisted and ended up with a six-foot-high fence that I later discovered chickens could easily fly over. I didn't know they could fly until then.

I made the best nesting area around with perches and nests with clean straw as shown in the book I bought "*Raising Chickens.*" I soon learned from the book, how to raise, butcher, and pluck chickens. With this newfound knowledge I drove to a large feed store in Napa and was swept away by the farminess of it all. The bulletin board showed wonderful things for sale like cows, pigs, goats and horses. I held my self back. First things first. But then I saw the baby chickens! Picture-book cute! All soft and fuzzy and peeping. I took home twenty five, along with the proper heat lamp, feeders and water dispensers. Chicks had to be kept warm and clean and not crowded. Where else but the kitchen? What fun watching the fuzz being replaced with feathers and eventually they were big enough to live in the coop I had made ready for them. The warm aroma of the heat lamp, chickens, and their feed filled our home with love.

Chopping Block

As they grew and filled the chicken yard, they started to crow. Only the roosters crowed, and I learned that when you buy chicks in bulk, they tend to be 75 % male.

This is where we butcher the roosters and eat them. No problem.

My tough, oldest son watched *The Waltons* and volunteered for the job. Terri held the poor chicken while Douglas held the axe. I stayed in the house.

Chickens really do run around for a while after their heads are off! The first one appeared to chase Chuck into the wood shed before it fell over.

It was unnerving for all of us, but we persevered and plucked and cleaned. I gutted as per the book's instructions and fried up a beautiful platter of chicken.

We sat around the table looking at it and finally piled into the car for the eight-mile trip to Mac Donald's.

I put the chicken book away and looked forward to hens laying eggs. Apparently there would be no chicken in our pot!

Classic Red

Roosters

After that fiasco I would only purchase sexed chicks which doubled the price and guaranteed only hens for egg laying, which was nice. If you ever wanted the hens to hatch baby chicks of their own though, you needed a rooster. Visions of a huge, grand rooster swirled through my head. I knew just what I wanted, a Rhode Island Red. It was named Rhode Island's state bird, so it had to be good. I bought a young one that looked like what I had pictured, and he grew to fit the picture perfectly. A beautiful red-bronze color with dark blue-black iridescent tail feathers that arched and cascaded like a glorious waterfall. His comb and wattles were thick and bright red; a sign of good health and virility. He was a dignified, magnificent, gentleman bird. Early each morning he produced a deep-throated vocalization to wake us up, and then proceeded to mate with every hen in the yard, which was in his job description. He would also make a certain clucking sound when he discovered something good to eat which he would share with his mates. He was a smart bird. I saw him chasing after a new hen and having no luck with the mating game. Then he causally strutted away, looked at the grass and clucked. When the silly hen ran over to see what tempting morsel he had discovered, he jumped on her, finished his business and coolly strutted away without a backward glance.

Chuck and Buckwheat

Buckwheat

I came home one afternoon to find we were dog owners. I had wondered what breed of dog would fit our needs, what color, and what sex. Well, those questions were all answered in the form of a small smoke- colored shivering creature named "Buckwheat", a male Weimaraner left by my husband's old girl friend on her way to live in the city. I never did like her.

"Just leave him on the back porch" the kids' father told us, "He will adjust."

Right. The poor guy was actually sucking on his paw and whimpering like the abandoned baby he was, although he looked about half my size. He slept with his warm body curled next to me that night and the next few until he was comfortable enough to take over the sofa. That didn't make Big Doug happy, but hey, it was his fault for accepting the dog without any discussion. He did adjust—the dog, not the man—and soon grew to the size of a small pony. Not only did he take over any sofa, he hogged the warmth of the fire in front of the fireplace!

Terri with ponies

Pony Ride

It used to be an old joke that every child asked for a pony for Christmas, and of course that was impossible. In Eden anything was possible; it just didn't always turn out like you had expected.

A friend of ours had recently moved to the country and acquired a few ponies because they "made the land look beautiful". When he discovered his folly he gave them away. We fell heir to a beautiful Shetland pony, whose back just came up to my waist, and her two-month-old

Buckwheat greets the pony

male offspring who was already bigger than she, and was still nursing. She was called a Palomino, which I learned was a color rather than a breed. She was a dark golden color with a creamy color mane and tail. She had a surly disposition which I later heard was common to the breed. Her son was a much lighter dusty gold color and had an air of cheerfulness about him. We were told his father was a horse, which may have explained his more pleasant disposition and size.

With dead pan humor, Big Doug unloaded the ponies and said, "Let's see how soon you can break these," referring to the short period of time most toys lasted.

No riding for now

We watched the animals grow and eat huge amounts of food daily. I became a frequent visitor to that feed store in Napa. Now I needed more bedding straw and bales of hay. I had dreams of pony rides and pony-cart parties. That little mare had ideas of her own. She would never accept a bit in her mouth, so we just placed a makeshift harness on her. I was too heavy for her—she was so small—but the kids tried riding her. She ran to the nearest tree, knowing how to remove any rider with a low-hanging branch. How do they know those things? Her son was friendlier, but we were told it would be at least two more years before he was old enough to ride.

By the way, breaking a horse, as in a rodeo, did not sound like anything I would attempt.

Oh, the joy of being up on a ladder picking fruit off your own tree and noticing a mare quietly sidling up to attempt to bite your leg or knock you off your perch! She never really did bite anyone, she just bared her teeth to watch us jump.

We built a wooden corral next to the barn. It looked great when we finished. I never realized how expensive the lowest grade two-by-fours could be. The ponies then spent their spare time chewing the fence. I didn't know horses would chew through wood. This whole thing was getting expensive, and it was hard work bringing in bales of hay. Ponies also required daily brushing and grooming and fly repellent, but they were so beautiful, their golden coats shining in the sun. They looked so graceful as they leapt over the fence to visit the neighbors. We didn't have a horse to follow them, and it could take all day coaxing them back on foot. I am glad we had understanding neighbors.

Love those chickens

Budding

By spring we really were country people. The golden hills turned emerald green with bouquets of golden poppies, purple lupine and clumps of bright yellow scotch broom making a live Easter picture for our personal viewing. It was easy to imagine what living in Ireland might look like. Various trees now were festooned with pink and white blossoms. I had yet to learn what fruit they might produce, but they looked like fairies in dancing dresses twirling all around us. To round out the picture our chickens, now full grown with beautiful red feathers, could be heard clucking proudly after laying their eggs. I soon learned to hurry and gather those eggs before the blue jays got to them, though. Those darn jays pecked the eggs open and ate them almost faster than I could run after I heard the hens cluck their special "I just laid an egg" cluck. The chickens wandered freely about cleaning the yards of all the bugs they could find. Sometimes I could see them on the farthest hill behind the house. I didn't realize sound could carry so far without houses and traffic in the way. They heard me calling "Hey chick, chick, chick!" I had treats of left over salads or store- bought corn for them daily, and they came jumping, flying and hopping to grab their share. I loved those chickens!

Chuck and some of his critters

Solitude

Chickens weren't the only ones who liked to venture up that tall hill. Douglas went just to scope things out, like a pioneer. He saw the remains of a reservoir and a rock formation at the very top that felt like a cave. It went in about four feet and provided a shelter from the sun. Terri went for the solitude—to be alone. She enjoyed occasionally escaping from the continuous chaos the boys created. Chuck took a lunch, his cat, and a transistor radio. Like Terri, he needed to get away once in a while, as long as he had music and, of course, a cat. David just trekked up and back, not liking to be alone much, but needing to say he did it.

In the spring, I, too, went to see what magic pulled them all up that hill. I trudged up, checking for rattle snakes along the way, as I had taught the kids to do. There was the cave—someone had left a pillow to sit on. I sat down and leaned my head back against a rock and instantly became the queen of Lilliput. I was a giant, observing the whole of it all, not just the bits and pieces of it. There was the tiny house, the road leading to it. It was plopped down in the middle of green-tinted, rounded, rolling hills, like a small boat in the ocean sinking in the waves. The splendor of the trees in blossom spread out around the perimeter. The chickens were scrambling dots, a child's miniature farm land. This viewpoint puts it all into perspective and renders the everyday problems small. I tried to maintain that feeling after I left.

Gardening

It was time to plant. I had already purchased my first *Farmer's Almanac* and eagerly consulted it. I certainly had enough space for a "kitchen garden" so I went to work. After digging for a few hours, I began to appreciate what the pioneers must have gone through. I was glad I wouldn't have to rely on my garden to see us through the next winter. The old half-collapsed barn out back had an intact floor covered with old compressed straw and manure, making it the best compost to be had. We shoveled and scraped and blended in a goodly portion along with the hand-plowed garden soil. This was to be the best organic garden. I ended up with a good-sized area with crooked rows of onions, radishes, lettuce and tomatoes—those being the hardiest and easiest for a beginner to raise. I had never seen lettuce growing before and could hardly wait to taste it fresh from the garden. Every day I watched as tiny, tender green shoots magically broke through the dirt, rising towards the sun. The green onions smelled so good I brushed the dirt off one and impulsively took a bite. I used no chemicals, no bug spray. That was the best bite of onion I ever had.

I saw the herd of deer from the bathroom window. They were wild and beautiful; they were eating my baby lettuce! By the time I ran around to the garden they were gone—as were the lettuce and tomatoes. They did leave the radishes and onions. I never attempted another garden. Unlike the pioneers, I had Safeway.

Oh, Nuts

Several trees with beautiful light pink blossoms began to develop what I soon realized must be almonds. Wow! I love almonds. What do people do with almonds? Off to the library again. Following the instructions, I waited until the outer shell was almost completely cracked open and spread a tarp under the tree. The kids and I then tried shaking the tree, even hitting it with a baseball bat, to make the almonds fall. We gathered our nuts and proceeded to the next tree. After a few trees, the thrill began to lessen.

Almond growers have drying trays. I had boxes and tarps and spread them out to dry in the sun. The birds eagerly gathered. I covered the nuts with fine chicken wire and still the birds, and now some squirrels came to sample almond smorgasbord. I set chairs out and had the boys take turns shooing the critters away with sticks. Of course they soon forgot the whole purpose of the assignment and started hitting each other. After the nuts were left over night, there wasn't much left to save. I brought some in and tried toasting them in the oven. Ugh, they tasted awful! The following years were easier, I just let the birds take care of it all. Since then, I only appreciate my almonds in Hershey bars.

Fruits of Our Labor

The fruit trees turned out to be cherry plums, for the most part, and were they good! There were tons of them! After the library trip, I learned to make plum jelly, plum jam, and plum pies. I got carried away making jelly and found mint growing around the side of the house, so I also made mint jelly. I made jelly out of everything I laid my hands on. I soon had stacks of jars glistening like jewels on the shelf, and I gave some as presents. The kids took boxes of the cherry plums down to the two lane road and set up a card table and a sign, proclaiming what a great deal for eating and cooking! They looked like poor farm kids in hopes of selling them and of course pocketing the profits. Not many cars came down that road, so soon it became boring. That might be why Doug decided that he needed that shiny post sticking in the ground next to a telephone pole that was about eight feet tall and being used as a fence post. According to his story later, he pulled and pulled and finally got his prize. He found out, too late, it was there to brace the fence post. The heavy fence post slammed down across his back bringing him to his knees, stunning him for a few minutes. When he could finally move again they all returned with the frightening story and never went back to the fruit business.

Outside Business

We were outside much of the time, so it was appropriate to have an outhouse. There had been the remains of an old outhouse behind the wood shed until Dave and a friend of his were found chopping away at it, each with a little axe. When questioned why they did such a thing their answer, "We needed the wood to build a chicken coop." Big Doug rebuilt the remaining wood structure, dug a hole under it, and poured a bag of lime in the hole. An old 12-inch television screen provided a window for light, and the obligatory lopsided half-moon was carved at the top of the door. It seemed like an added luxury since we had indoor plumbing. It was a one holer without a catalog. You can only go so far with re-creating' the old days. It came in handy many times, although I believe Terri never went near it.

Tranquility

Ol' Water Hole

If we only had a pond, this place would look like the Garden of Eden. We certainly had enough room for one. So that first summer we all took up shovels and started in digging. It was a lot of work, and soon the dimensions we first planned began to shrink. After a few weeks, we gave in and called it completed. Not bad. It was approximately ten by ten and five feet deep. Okay, so we didn't work every day.

We joyfully turned on the hose and, though it took a long time, filled it up. I'd been told we didn't have to worry about a water bill; we had our own well. I never had any indication of where that well was located. Certainly that old hand pump standing near the house was not attached to one. I gave it no further thought.

We brought out aluminum, woven, folding chairs and sat around our pond that we built. What a joyous feeling of accomplishment. Within a couple of days the water was almost gone. What's the difference between a natural pond and one you create? We left the hose on a slow drip after refilling it and that took care of the problem. I did worry when told that wells do occasionally dry up in the summer. Do they give advance warning or just stop? I got lucky on this one, and we made it through the summer just fine. The boys jumped in and splashed around at first. They even cut lengths of hose, put their heads under water and tried to snorkel. However, once ducks had made the pond their home, the boys stopped this practice.

.

Drink of Life

Speaking of wells, I had presumed we would have the healthiest water to be found until we started having intestinal distress. I took a sample of our water to the agriculture department in Fairfield and the test results found it to be not especially safe for drinking a fact which, the kids' father never did believe, and he never seemed sick. For the rest of us, I always carried empty containers when I went visiting friends and relatives and brought back city tap water which we used for drinking and cooking, leaving the well water for all other purposes.

.

Ducks Galore

 Douglas came in one day after school started and proudly held out four fuzzy baby ducks.

"This kid brought them to "Show-and-Tell" 'cause he found them on the water front. I told him they would die if I didn't bring 'em home 'cause my mom knows how to raise and feed them."

I did? Out came the chicken warmer and feeder. I whipped up a combination of goose and baby chicken food, and they seemed to do well. We soon had Mallard ducks bobbing and splashing in our pond.

Goosed

I soon realized I needed a goose. A baby, of course. I drove all over Napa looking and found only one place with goslings. They were an Asian family that raised Chinese geese to eat, and it took a lot of persuading to talk them into selling one small live goose exactly one day old. It was twice as big as a baby chicken and even cuddlier. Although its food requirements were somewhat different, I set to the task. I boiled eggs and mixed them with bread crumbs and various other things, getting more help from the library. That baby goose was so cute following us around the house; it would become frantic, chirping wildly and flapping its little stubs of featherless wings if we were out of sight. Baby chickens never acted like that. I put it under the heat lamp that night and went to bed, but it started chirping like it was being killed. It didn't have any other chicks to cuddle with! Yes, of course I took it to bed with me wrapped in a light blanket, and it slept well. I had a harder time sleeping for fear of hurting it. The next night Douglas slept with Homer, as we named him, and every night from then on, and kissed him goodnight on his little beak until one night Homer bit his lip. By then the goose was big enough to sleep alone and happily joined the ducks in the pond. He was a great watch dog, shrilly calling out if someone was approaching the house before we saw or heard anything. One day he came out from the bush where he had been resting, and left behind a gigantic egg. We decided he must, in fact, be a she. We renamed her "Goosey". She left us an egg every month for a while. We tried making omelets from them and though they tasted fine, it just didn't seem right, somehow.

Dave, Chuck and Doug

Sheba, David and Buckwheat

Sheba

Too bad I read *Heidi* when I was young because the idea of raising goats sounded like fun the more I thought about it. Now I spent my spare time checking out goat farms in Napa. That was really fun! It was spring, and the farms had barns full of mother goats with their new offspring. Goats usually have twins. When they are born they bounce around and act like puppies with hooves. Their eyes are open, and they are on their feet within minutes after they are born. I watched them being bottle-fed since they were

Douglas sharing a mouthful

bred to be milked. As they did with cattle, farmers kept only one male, and he was a smelly, disgusting guy. The babies and females had a nice earthy smell that I liked right away.

I came home with a year-old white female with long hair, a beautiful Angora that we named "Sheba". This goat was a great deal since she wasn't a baby, and of a breed that didn't produce milk well. I never planned on milking her. What a joy she was, and she didn't have to sleep in the house! She'd follow me around in the yard all day and then she went into the barn at night. I had fixed a nice place for her with straw where she spent the night. Of course, when I bought the straw I also included hay and special feed for goats. Oh, and a special brush to keep that long, white hair looking good.

Getting acquainted

Feed me more!

More goats

Not very heavy

Bottle-feeding time

Enter the Boys

A few months later an old friend showed up with a present: two baby goats! I told Buckwheat he had to stay in the house so he wouldn't scare them. He was a very excitable pooch. The kids and I greeted the most adorable brown and white male goats. We were shown how to feed them with a huge nipple (found in feed stores) stretched over a coke bottle filled with milk. We got them all settled in the barn with their new friend Sheba and returned to the house to find Buckwheat sitting in the living room chewing on one thing that he found from each bedroom, a shoe, a slipper, a toy, and a baseball mitt. Who says dogs don't try to punish their owners?

Later, the kids and I built ramps and made a play yard for those babies. Goats of any age love to jump on and off ramps of any kind, including any car in the driveway, which we tried to discourage. Big Doug didn't always appreciate the cuteness of it. Those babies grew so fast, they were soon eating on their own. I was glad they didn't smell like I thought all male goats did.

One morning while walking past the barn I heard an odd bird song and looked into the barn. It wasn't a bird; it was the bleat of a newborn baby goat! Oh my gosh, my white goat, Sheba, had just given birth and was busy cleaning her baby while it was trying to get to its feet for the first time. As I watched in amazement she delivered baby number two. Two white kids, one boy and one girl! She thankfully delivered them safely without my help. I wasn't even aware she was expecting! All goats are barrel shaped anyway and who was the father? Could it be one of my males? I didn't know they could be fathers at only six months! The mother fed these babies and they were soon running on the ramps and bouncing off the walls. I mean literally: they would run to the wall, take a step up, and bounce off. Nothing is more fun than a goat unless it's five of them.

Sheba and new babies

Kids at play

Crossing the Line

Everyone has different fantasies; mine was to have a pulley clothesline. Where we had temporarily lived before there was no yard, and the kids and I had trekked baskets of clothes to the laundromat every Sunday.

Now I had acres of land. My father-in-law had built sturdy lines for me in the past and I tried to live up to my mother-in-law's expectations that a woman was judged by how early her wash was hung out on the line. So by six in the morning I had had line after line of diapers snapping smartly in the wind.

Now, having the luxury of older kids and neighbors too far away to judge, I could indulge in a pulley line and never leave my back porch. It ran from the porch to the side of the wood shed.

There is something very gratifying to see your sheets and such flapping in the breeze. Until, that is, you see the goat pulling at your laundry. Even the goose joined in the game of grab-the-sheets. The fun was over (for them) after the line was adjusted to a higher level.

.

What's That Smell?

We were surrounded by three hundred acres of rolling hills and cattle-grazing land. If the cattle came too close to the yard I would yell to Buckwheat, "Sic-um!" and he would happily chase them away. He acted like a regular farm dog running after them, barking, with a big grin on his doggie face. Maybe that's what started him chasing things. There wasn't a fence enclosing the yard, and I just couldn't tie a dog up, so after Buckwheat spent the night out a few times, I would try to keep a careful watch on him when he went outside. The minute I glanced away, he was off, and once started, he wouldn't stop even though he heard me call. He would look back and keep running.

"Fine," I thought, "stay out, and don't come back!" He always came back around three or four in the morning smelling like skunk! "Oh, No!" I yelled at him. "Stay out!" He would whine and cry and scratch at the door and wake up everyone, so I had no choice but to let him in, put him in the bathtub and bathe him with strawberry shampoo to kill the smell. That went on almost every night for a while. To this day that strawberry scent smells like skunk to me.

Spreckles and family

More Soft and Fuzzy

Ah, spring, when a cat's fancy turns to love. The cats were meowing to go out at night, and suitors lined up outside ready to escort them on a romantic walk in the woods. Where did they all come from? I conquered for a time, determined not to let them out, but then I lost this battle, too.

Weeks later Chuck woke me saying, "There's something wet on my bed", and there was our cat having kittens in his bed. Yes, he slept with the cats. We made a bed in his closet for mother and babies and observed a colorful miracle while she delivered several more. She was a wonderful mother with orange, black, and mixed-color kittens.

A few days later her sister had kittens in the porch laundry sink, and then moved the poor things one by one from one place to another until finally satisfied. She often wandered off and stayed away too long. Not all cats were meant to be mothers.

Our family room soon became a riot of activity, color, and shredded curtains. It was difficult to count the many balls of fur running under and over the sofa. It was fun, but all good things must come to an end. We found good homes for them, keeping the mothers and one orange guy. The cats would occasionally bring in a dead creature for us to admire, some almost as big as the cat herself. I wondered, did she kill it or find it this way and bring it back to impress us? Things I never knew existed found its way to our back porch. For example, I had never seen a mole before. It struck me that she would hunt and retrieve wild things, but she never brought in or even chased any animal or chicken or duck, grown or baby, from our yard.

Henry posing with Sam, the cat

Henry and Bear

During this time we acquired two more dogs. One pup was found running on the street in town and rescued, another given by the SPCA. That little pup later named "Henry", looked like poodle mix, and Chuck loved him. That pup would run through the fields, and you couldn't see him until he came in crying and scratching his ears. Fox tails! We were taking a trip to the vet two or three times a week for several weeks when the vet suggested a new home for this poor guy. He wasn't the kind of dog for this rough way of life.

The other was a German Shepherd named "Bear" given to us by the SPCA. However, that dog was too much of a handful for me to train. I never could house-break him or walk him on a leash. I watched him and Buckwheat catching mice. He would position himself at one end of a patch of muddy ground with Buckwheat maybe twenty feet away at the other end. I swear they watched each other, then Buckwheat would nod and the Shepherd would start frantically digging, which caused the mouse to burrow towards Buckwheat who snatched it up, and it was gone in a blink. I know the Shepherd was smart, but it was the other guy who always got the mouse. I found a young couple (the husband had just been drafted) and she wanted the dog for security while he was gone, so the Shepherd had a new home.

Guns—more problems on the farm

You'll Shoot your Eye Out

I had not believed in having guns up to this time, and then the boys were given BB guns for Christmas. I gave in slightly and allowed target shooting. No bird or animal was to be injured by this family! If we lived in the old days and had to hunt to survive, we would. Now we buy meat at the supermarket.

I set up paper targets against bales of straw, and they had fun with target practice. It wasn't until years later I was told the boys, at least once, stuck plywood under their shirts and shot at each other! I would have taken those guns away if I had known that then.

We had a locked gun cabinet containing two rifles, and I also had a small hand gun. I set tin cans on straw bales with empty fields behind them, hung targets from trees, and became a pretty fair marksman. Although I never have been a great proponent of gun ownership, I feel it becomes important when you live out like we were for an added sense of security. Since Terri was the oldest, I tried to convince her to try shooting in case there was an emergency, but she refused, saying she would never shoot anyone, even to save a life. Given half a chance, Douglas would have shot whatever moved. Kids all have their own personalities, no matter how they are raised.

Who Was It?

One Saturday morning the kids were all piled on my bed talking and kidding around when we saw a shadow on the bedroom window. It was at the end of the porch and the shade was pulled down so no one could see in, not that we thought that was a possibility. It was only there for an instant then gone; however we had clearly seen the outline of a head wearing what looked like a cowboy hat. It took a frozen second to respond, then I called the sheriff, grabbed my gun, and told the kids to stay put. I went outside carefully looking around—prepared to shoot first and ask questions later. There were so many places to hide, but luckily I never found anyone. The sheriff came right away and said he thought he had heard a gunshot on the way and asked if it was me! It wasn't. Thankfully that was the only intruder experience we had.

Poor Bird

One morning when I was sleeping in Terri came and woke me saying a poor blue jay was suffering and could I help. I went out to see a large blue jay with huge eyes blinking at me and obviously mortally wounded. I would rather put something out of its misery than watch it suffer.

What to do, though? I couldn't just hit it with a hammer or something awful like that, so I went in and got my gun. I pointed it down towards the bird lying on the sidewalk and pictured the bullet bouncing off the cement and hitting me. So I lay down next to the bird where I couldn't miss and pulled the trigger.

My world turned black; I couldn't hear for the ringing in my ears. I couldn't open my eyes because they were stuck shut. I wiped the mess off with my hand and saw the bird was gone. I realized I was wearing it! My hair, my face, and nightgown were covered with blood and feathers. My mood was black, too, when I picked myself up to take a shower and snapped at the kids not to wake me again if I am sleeping!

Green Eggs and Ham

We met neighbors who lived on the other side of the hill, an older couple with a pronounced southern drawl who were renting a small three-room shack. They told us of their plan to return to Texas while they sat next to a small wood-burning stove in the middle of the tiny living room. An empty string bean can sat next to the stove, and into this can the old lady spit tobacco while animatedly discussing crocheting. She fashioned her delicate yarn in a loop around an old broom stick down each row, creating a light, airy, beautiful piece of work! These bed coverings looked rather incongruous in the primitive cabin setting.

The old man offered to leave us his livestock, which consisted of a beef cow and her calf and several chickens they claimed laid blue eggs. The chickens had no house, nests or food. They roosted in the trees and just lived a wild life. There is no way to run around and catch chickens. When they roost, they are easy prey. That was how I was able to sprinkle mite powder on mine. Just like flea powder on a dog, chickens need to be treated also. In the close quarters of a chicken house after dark, this is just not fun. For these wild hens, we had to bring cages and ladders and come back at night to pluck them off their tree perches. Once they were brought in with the others at our place, they adjusted immediately. And yes, they laid light blue and green eggs.

The cow and calf came home to us in the back of our pickup which had tall side panels. It was like a rodeo trick catching the calf, tossing a rope around it for a collar and then it was easy enough to lead him. Wherever you take the calf, the cow will follow, so up the ramp, into the truck, with me trying to keep them calm on the ride home. Yes, me in the back between two big animal bumping into me around every turn in the road! That was an experience I will not soon forget.

Kick the Bucket

Now I had a cow I could milk! She wouldn't be as productive as a Guernsey or a Jersey, but she was free. So back to Napa I went for bales of hay and a very expensive, special bucket just for milking cows. No seams where bacteria could collect, very shiny and expensive. I tried to wean the calf on the first day of the new moon. Old farmers say that practice never fails. *Farmer's Almanac* agreed. I guess the calf never read that part. I thought it would be cruel to separate the calf from her mother for too long a period, so we never had an overabundance of milk. It was a real learning experience. I tied her in an enclosed area, washed her teats, placed the bucket under her and knew the joy of hearing milk hitting the bucket. I quickly found it was very tiring to hands not used to such activity. About the time I was getting tired, she put her foot in the bucket. That milk was thrown out, the beautiful bucket washed, and we tried again. Over time I gave up this frustrating practice, after I had made the best butter you ever tasted and obtained bragging rights to having milked a cow.

It seemed a battle of wits or control, each time I had to walk this cow to the barn, pasture or anywhere she preferred not to go. Sometimes she would break into a trot to try to shake me loose. She had been on her own much too long. I just held onto that rope and let my weight tire her out while she dragged me across the yard, with my heels digging in the dirt. What a sight we must have been. I was determined and finally won and we continued our walk with me in the lead, at a much slower pace.

.

Released

The people in Vallejo bought two cute baby chicks for their kids at Easter and put an ad in the paper months later selling them. Poor Salt and Pepper! Those black and white chicks had grown into big hens that could hardly fit in the same cage together anymore. When I took them home and opened the cage, they hesitated leaving the only home they knew and then stepped out and touched grass for the first time, shook themselves, and flew a few feet into the air. I would describe their behavior as ecstatic.

.

Burial Grounds

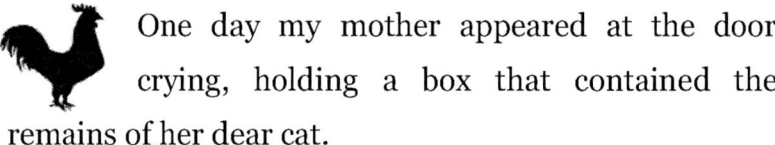One day my mother appeared at the door crying, holding a box that contained the remains of her dear cat.

" I didn't know where else to take him," she sobbed.

That was the beginning of The Pet Cemetery. Living in the country has a down side. Things die from natural and often unnatural causes. People tend to drop unwanted pets out in the country near a farm, assuming they will fend and forage for themselves or be taken in by farm people. I have tried to coax kittens and cats to me and put out food for them, only to find their little dead bodies later. Kittens, rabbits, chickens and more were interred in our ever expanding "place of eternal rest". The kids placed little crosses made of popsicle sticks and flowers at the grave and said a little prayer for each animal.

Integration

Animal behavior is a subject I was beginning to find increasingly interesting. Any chickens I brought home from other places never ran off, and I turned them all free to do so if they wanted. They seemed to know safety was in a group, so they readily joined the others in search of tasty morsels or just milled around waiting for me to come out and toss them something. However, they were a family within a family with the Reds grouped together, the wild ones in a separate group, and any others I later introduced forming their own group. Salt and Pepper ran shoulder-to-shoulder when keeping up with the rest. Different breeds kept this separate-but-together behavior. A beautiful golden, tiny Bantam rooster and hen kept close contact like an old married couple. We also had a few Japanese Silkies that appeared to have long white hair instead of feathers and their skin was black, not yellow.

We had a routine that we followed, and the chickens had no objections. At dusk they all went into the roomy hen house, and I locked them in for the night and let them out first thing in the morning. New comers just followed along. One day a friend gave me her six Guinea Hens. These are beautifully marked birds with homely faces; they originated in Africa. The first night I called them, tried to herd them, and failed in my attempts to persuade them to join the others in the hen house. "No", they seemed to say, "We are wild, we roost in trees". I didn't hear anything in the night, but bloody feathers under the tree told the story. Two were never seen again. That night the Guinea Hens that were spared lined up with the other birds outside the hen house and quickly ran inside. No more tree roosting for them. I have heard that chickens and other birds are stupid. I have only seen evidence to the contrary.

Bad Rooster

I do think it might have been my fault that the rooster was so mean. Big Red owned his harem of red hens. The Silky rooster had his, as did the bantam and others. This bad rooster, though, was a beautiful golden rooster, and where he came from I have forgotten. He would try to mate with other hens and was chased away. He even tried to mount a Guinea hen who only shook him off. I really didn't think much about him until he started attacking David. I don't remember anyone else complaining. I told David he was much bigger than a bird, so he just should not allow the rooster to attack him. Finally he started carrying a stick every time he went outside, but even then that darn rooster would keep flying at him. It did look comical. When that rooster flew at him, bird and boy both looked about the same size, and I think David didn't really want to hurt him, so this behavior continued for some time.

Douglas coming...

Going...(but mostly off)

Giddi-up

Since the boys couldn't ride the ponies, Douglas tried his hand at riding at calf- riding when the calf was half grown. I think the pony had given the cow advice, since the calf headed for the nearest tree to dislodge his rider. Chuck tried riding when no one was around to laugh, and the calf was in the corral. It headed right to fence and rubbed him off. Neither Douglas or Chuck tried again. Terri and David wisely declined the offer to try to ride.

Sorry, Terri

The boys were outside a lot being cowboys or farmers or whatever was the topic of the day, and I really thought Terri should feel the fulfillment of outdoor work and adventure, too. To that end, I insisted she would have fun joining me in tearing down an old barn. Only one wall and most of the floor was left, affording us plenty of sunshine. I even let her use my favorite crowbar while I used the hammer to pull those old boards apart. Some of the nails were round, and in a few places, wooden pegs had been used.

The joy of accomplishment, feeling your muscles work, smelling the tree-scented air—these are the feelings I wanted to impart to her. I think we may have enjoyed those things for about fifteen minutes when she screamed that she had stepped on a nail!

Oh, in my rush to help her, I started climbing down the ladder I was on, and quickly hung my hammer on a board. The hammer then slipped and fell, hitting her on the head! I didn't know which to look at first, the nail in her foot or the huge lump swelling under her hat.

That was it! I never could convince her to join us working outside after that. Undoubtedly, that was a smart move on her part.

We finished off the barn by wrapping rope around some boards holding up the side wall and securing the rope to the bumper of the old truck. I now can picture what might have happened if those boards had come loose sailing through the air towards us or ripping the bumper off. Instead it was quite exciting watching that huge expanse of rotten wood swaying back and forth and finally crashing to the ground in a cloud of dust. We all cheered and, thankfully, remained unscathed.

Cattle Auction

One day an acquaintance happily brought us two baby calves. It only took a day to realize these poor guys were not going to make it. I called the fellow to come and get them and take them where more experienced people could care for them.

Shortly afterwards, I attended my first cattle auction. What an eye-opener. The announcer told everyone why they should only raise and eat their own beef. I never knew such things about the meat industry. I also saw why those little steers I was given probably wouldn't make it. They had a pen of the sickly creatures that were sold to make dog food, which is a good idea for the ranchers and the dogs, however not for me. I never went back.

Bandit and I

Bandit

I was a bit skeptical when the people over the hill offered us a hand-raised calf whose mother had died birthing it. It was only one month old, and its back barely came up past my knees. She did appear strong and sturdy; they insisted it would survive and showed me how to feed it. They had bottle-fed the first month and now were in the process of weaning the calf. They gave me a wash tub full of milk, showed me how to put my hand under the milk and let the calf suck .

Douglas with Bandit

on my fingers while slowly pulling them under, so she actually drinking from the tub. Clever.

When a calf nurses and the milk isn't forthcoming, nature tells it to butt the mother's utter to help things along. With a wet milky face this calf would butt me on the chest and knock me over. I learned to put on old clothes and embrace this experience several times a day. In time she did learn to drink by herself. I learned too, not to accept another cow. She was a black-and-white beef cow with markings on her face like a mask, so the kids named her "Bandit" and she followed me around like the rest of the critters and grew huge.

She was tame and easily moved from one area to the next. Of course water has to be moved also. The first time I bent over to pick up the water pan I saw the shadow of a huge cow coming down over me and jumped back just in time. She was fond of trying to embrace me from the back. I had to watch carefully or risk being flattened. I guess we really bonded.

Just Like Kittens

I can't believe after my experience with the chickens I would consider rabbits. Just think, you can eat them and sell the skins. I had eaten rabbit when I was younger; it tasted like chicken. There were old rabbit hutches waiting to be repaired and used. I started with a pair, keeping them separate except for mating, like the book said. Good way for the kids to learn the facts of life too, when they put the male in with the female for mating. Sure enough, the babies came in thirty days and the mother took good care of them. They were like kittens, so fuzzy and cute as shown in Easter pictures. I put a colorful sign on the road advertising bunnies for sale. Some folks dropped by to buy butchered rabbits, and of course, I turned them down. Our rabbits were only sold as pets. We soon had more rabbits, and more rabbits, and more. Rabbits eat a lot of food. I had thirty-gallon cans of chicken food, rabbit food, dog and cat food, and stacks of hay and straw. I did feel good that nothing was wasted in our house. All leftovers went to the animals, mostly the chickens, who loved these treats.

By this time, I began to realize country living was more work than I had planned on. Oh, I guess I never did plan, did I? I now needed to frequently travel to Napa to stock up on bales of hay, sacks of various feeds, and supplies. These things were heavy! I also had to feed and water and keep all these animals clean. Every day!

Dave with Red Rabbit

Lucky Truck ?

I brought David his own bunny, a beautiful little rabbit with red-colored fur. He loved it and kept it separate from the run-of-the-mill rabbits. When he was home one day and the others were in school, we made a special trip to town just for a salt lick for his rabbit.

Thank God it was hot, and the old farm truck had no air conditioner, requiring us to keep our windows open. It also had no seat belts. Nobody had seat belts back then. As I rounded a turn onto the country road for the trip home, the old door on David's side of the truck flew open. He grabbed that window frame, still clutching that paper bag containing the salt lick, and held on as the door swung wide. I quickly braked and pulled him back in and kept him near me for the rest of the trip. If that window hadn't been down, if he hadn't held on like a little monkey, he would have rolled out and maybe been run over. So many ifs in life! I just thanked God for the way things turned out.

Sweetie Face

By now I should have been content with the animals we had already acquired, but no, an English bull dog would be so cute. For once, Napa was not the place to look. Internet wasn't invented yet, so I traveled within a fifty-mile radius and finally found Sweetie Face. She was white with some black markings, and the breeder in Sacramento gave me a good deal. She was a good dog who spent her time mostly curled up sleeping and resembled a plump marshmallow with black eyes. I don't remember her even walking outside, although she must have.

When she was old enough I found a handsome male for her to have a family with. However, neither of them were interested. The vet tried artificial insemination, for a price of course. It did not work. I finally let the breeder I got her from place her into a horrible sling so she would accept her lover's advances. I didn't stay to watch. I felt like such a traitor.

She came home expecting. After sixty days she started labor and it became apparent she was having trouble, so we were off to the vet as soon as they opened. They informed me a cesarean would take place at lunch time. I called my breeder who wanted it dome immediately for the sake of the mother and puppies. She was ready to sue the vet if he waited. He was not impressed by this threat, and we did wait until lunch time.

The first pup was deceased, the remaining four were healthy. English bulldogs die easily. If the mother woke alone she might pant until her throat swelled shut, so I told the vet I was taking her home.

"She should spend the night," he told me.

I asked if anyone would be with her at night.

"No," he informed me. "I have a life other then here."

My mother and I boxed up the tiny babies and I carried the heavy, still-sleeping new mother and laid her on the front seat of my truck, leaving my own poor mother to climb over the rusted-shut tail gate into the back for the ride home.

I spent the night watching Sweetie Face so she did not choke. I fed the new pups every couple of hours, putting a small tube down their throats with formula, praying I would not kill them. After each feeding a warm, wet cloth in place of a mother's tongue facilitated their bowel and urinary functions.

Bulldog pups

When the new mother woke in the morning she refused to nurse, leaving me to sit with her and the pups for the next three days to make sure she stayed with them. She never did bond with them, and my breeder un-bonded with me when I confessed I had Sweetie Face fixed so that neither she nor I would experience another ordeal like that.

We kept one male puppy and sold the other three. We didn't make a profit, but we at least got a little back.

Adventurers

"Let's walk in the woods," I told the kids. The fields beyond the house rippled in the breeze. The house appeared to sit in the middle of the ocean. The air was warm and scented, the sky a hazy blue with a few scattered white clouds. Who wouldn't want to be out in nature? Walking through this pretend sea was more difficult than I thought though, and it was hot in the full sun. Terri was the first to turn around and go back.

"You'll miss all the fun." I called after her. She never looked back. I don't think she even heard me. "Well, maybe we will see a beehive; listen, you can hear their buzzing." I encouraged what remained of my troops. There was a steady drone in the air, but luckily we never found the source.

Like prairie people of old, we came across bleached bones of creatures that had been there before us. They looked like cow bones, but you never know. It was cooler in among the trees and so adventuresome. When we came to a slight drop-off leading to a creek I thought it would be safer to slide down, and I grabbed a handful of weeds to slow my descent. That's how I discovered stinging nettle. My whole hand and wrist felt like it was on fire! It burned like a hundred bee stings! I stuck my hand in the mud of the creek. Isn't that what the settlers and Indians did? If so, it isn't much help. I was looking at my hand when a bee became tangled in one of two pony tails keeping my hair in place.

"Douglas," I screamed, and he started clapping at my hair bravely, trying to dislodge the bee.

Chuck and David jumped around in response, and David yelled "I'm gonna go get Terri!"

I called him back; the bee went away without stinging Douglas or me. We turned and went home, a dirty faced, silent, subdued group of pioneers, unrecognizable from the high spirited adventurers that set off on their journey earlier that morning. I spent the evening with my hand elevated in ice packs. That was our last "Into The Woods" adventure.

Road falling into creek

All Wet

By our second season in the country, we were used to the roads collapsing in the rain. This time, however, it flooded. The field on the low side of the house turned into a lake. The stream that had dried up in the summer became a raging river. The water covered the low points of Lake Herman Road, not allowing the school bus access for days. The kids stood waiting in the mud for twenty minutes before realizing the bus was not coming. The flood cut us off from the outside world for a few days.

Fields flooding by the house and over the road

Archie Bread

What is more enticing than the aroma of home-baked bread filling the country kitchen? The kids could smell bread baking before they reached the house after school and would come in shouting, "Archie bread!"

Archie, in his late seventies, was a frequent visitor. He was drawn to the country as we were drawn to his baking, and he had fun joining us in whatever work was in progress. He helped us repair fences and sheds, and warned us of the dangers of hawks. He had noticed them flying overhead and told us that one day they would swoop down and grab a chicken. That never did happen, though I am sure it might have in the old days.

He had been a baker in the merchant marines long ago. He would share stories of the old days while he mixed the dough, let it rise on the stove, and then bake mouth-watering rolls and loaves of bread. He was expected at our house when illness overtook him.

He sent a letter from the hospital that he would be coming when he was better. When I hadn't heard in a couple of weeks we inquired and learned sadly that he had passed on. Although we never saw him again we will never forget him.

Dive in the Hive

While we didn't find a bee hive in the woods, we discovered one in the tin shed at edge of the line of outbuildings. It was huge, stuck up in the corner, with honeybees all over it! How to get the honey? Didn't the pioneers smoke them out? I decided the best way was to set a fire in a wash tub to contain it, and add an old tire for smoke. It did smoke for a long time. The bees saw me strike the first match and swarmed on me! I ran sooo fast and jumped into that homemade duck pond up to my neck! I was stung about seven times, mostly on my arms, before the bees went away. I felt slightly sick that night and sicker still when later I found there was no honey in that hive. No wonder pioneers died at young ages.

Not Lit Up

Actually, there were many times that potentially harmful things happened while we were in the country. One fine morning I discovered we had no electricity! I went around trying various lights: nothing. Then I went outside and discovered the cause: an electrical line was down laying across the front yard where kids, dogs or anything could have wandered over it. I was smart enough to leave it alone and call the electric company.

A worker who looked like he was in his forties came right out, looked at it and with a shake of his head informed me "It ain't one of ours, you gotta get an electrician out here."

I never dreamed electric lines belonged to anyone! Seeing the dismay on my face he slyly looked up at me and said, "we could work out a deal, though, what with you, a pretty little thing, being out here all alone."

He only thought I was alone. I had kids and a gun. I saw him off the property! An electrician got it fixed in no time before anyone stepped on it!

A Break in the Wood Shed

Maybe if other children hadn't been visiting, this might never have happened. They were chasing each other around, and when Chuck ran in the woodshed they thought it fun to lock him in. He knew what to do; he had seen cowboy movies where the fellow climbed up into the rafters of a barn and climbed out the little window in the top. So he piled up enough wood to climb up on the exposed beam that ran across the top to a small loft and window. Unfortunately, too late, he noticed the two-by-four was not nailed down and just balanced on brackets, allowing the board to fall before he reached his goal, and sending him about ten feet to the floor. That's when the kids opened the door.

I only found out about it when he calmly walked into the house holding his arm and stated, "I think I broke my arm." That was an understatement. His arm looked like a wash board, was broken in several places, and had a piece of bone protruding through. A quick trip to the hospital, general anesthesia and an overnight stay was required to fix the problem. I don't think he ever cried.

Chuck outside the infamous woodshed

Sam

Chuck had a new white cast and a release from school for a few weeks. He proudly wore the slings I made for him decorated with patterns of cars and cowboys. He joined me when I went to visit a friend who raised lantern-eyed cats. Since he was a wounded warrior, he got to pick out and name a new kitten. He happily tucked it safely into his sling for the ride home and named him "Sam". Cats always did take to Chuck.

Look Out, Mouse

It was probably Chuck who saved the little mouse's life. As Chuck started to enter the family room, he saw two dogs and three cats sitting in a semi-circle staring intently at a small mouse in front of the fireplace. It was a game of intense stare-down with obvious winners. Not wanting to see the end of this story, he started to leave which broke the spell just for a second, giving that lucky mouse time to escape. It ran into the fireplace and down the ash clean-out which lead to the basement where, I am sure, he joined his family and friends.

That's Scary

I knew it was a bad sign when one of the hens didn't appear to enter the coop for the night. Sometimes wild ways would overcome them, and they would sit on a nest hidden the bushes instead the hen house. It was not safe to be out at night, and I looked all around for her with a heavy heart. When I heard her scream in the middle of the night, I wasn't surprised. The noise came from close by my bedroom, so I ran out onto the porch hoping to scare whatever it was away in time to save her. I yelled the same sound I might yell at the cows in the road, kind of a "Ya, Ya!"

Something screamed back at me, a mocking "Ya, Ya!" sound! If the devil himself had appeared out of the darkness I couldn't have been more shocked! Something came to stand right below me with only the solid porch separating us. It rocked from side to side staring up at me with fierce glowing eyes. I had no doubt it wanted to attack me too and just couldn't figure out how. I ran and woke the kids' father who got the gun and came right out. It was still standing there waiting. He took a quick shot and missed! It then took off and I only saw a shadow outline of something that looked as big as a German shepherd.

I hunted around for the nest the next morning and never found a feather or egg shell, but the poor chicken never came back. Whatever it was got what it wanted. A few days after that I heard what sounded like a cat in heat near the back porch, a low yowling sound. I peeked out and saw the ducks nervously swimming in the middle of the pond, and knew it was not anything friendly. I inquired at the Agricultural Center if it could have been a wild cat of some kind and was told yes, even wolves were a possibility where I lived. Animals apparently can follow the mountain range from the north. The picture of Eden changed somewhat in my mind after that, and if I went out at night I always had a gun in my pocket.

Chuck with next resident of the Pet Cemetery

Shocking

Sometimes disaster strikes even when you think you are prepared. I heard the squawks as I neared the hen house to let them out in the early morning. As I entered, I stepped into bloody chaos. Roosters and hens struggling to reach the highest perches were saved while hens that were sheltering chicks and couldn't get away were torn apart along with their babies. A massacre, a slaughter that appeared more for fun than food, for the perpetrator was still present! A huge raccoon had ripped pieces of wood of the back of the shed enough to squeeze in!

I love and respect all life forms, but this horrible act could not be ignored. His end came swiftly with a bullet to the head. He and what remained of my deceased, precious babies and their mothers went to join others in our Pet Cemetery.

Sadness

Sad things happened in runs and then slacked off for a while. Someone gave me two small chickens that could be outdoors; they just needed time to adjust to the others, so I placed them in a bottomless cage so they were able to eat grass and scratch. They lasted one day. I discovered they had disappeared and saw the hole in the ground under the cage. I never knew if it was a snake or mole or something else that took them away.

I was given two small Pencil Runner ducks that walked almost upright and were fun to watch. I found one tangled up in weeds, unfortunately deceased, and never located the other. Two small peacocks never got a chance to make loud screaming noises as adults because they disappeared after two days. I hadn't realized the bucolic country setting harbored so many predators.

Snakes

We saw plenty of snakes around the house. The smaller ones the boys found swimming in the steam were nothing compared to the huge snakes on the sidewalks and patches of dirt around the house. So common were they that we had to watch our feet in the spring and summer for fear of stepping on one.

The first one I saw was around five feet long with a tan-colored body and dark brown blotches. I was afraid it might be a rattlesnake. It coiled back into a striking position, its head flattened and hissing loudly, its tail shaking, making a rattling sound. But it was a fake. It didn't have any rattles. On investigation it turned out to be a California Gopher Snake.

I cannot guess how many hid in grasses around the house. We saw them mostly in twos wrapped around the length of each other in what I supposed was a mating ritual. The dog sniffed at them, but they never took notice, so he left them alone. As long as they weren't rattlers, I was happy to have them around to keep down the rodent population.

A Wolf ?

I could barely see them from the house, so I drove the truck down the road to an old barn to be sure. I was almost afraid they were a pair of wolves. I had seen so much by now, nothing would surprise me. I watched from the safety of my truck for a few minutes and finally worked up the nerve to confront two beautiful Siberian Huskies. They had on collars hidden in that fur and happily went home with me to eat large amounts of dog food. After much long distance calling, thanks to the tags on the collars, I located the owner. He told me a story of having been in the process of moving from another state to San Francisco when he stopped his jeep on my road for a nap and woke to discover his dogs missing. He came and picked them up and gave me a small plant for my trouble. I hope he watched them more closely after that.

Doggie Problems

The kids were piling into the car for a ride to school. We had just started down the lane when I thought I heard the goats bleating and went back to look. There was Buckwheat having a great time, grabbing at the goats' ears with his teeth. Even though I had allowed their horns to grow, they were unable to defend themselves! He had purposely waited until we left to start the harassment. I had to secure him now before I went anywhere.

When Douglas's grandparents drove up to take him to church, Buckwheat got so excited he raised his leg as he ran to greet the car and wet all over Douglas's suit.

Another time when Terri took a shortcut through an opening in the hedge to reach the road on her way to school he ran past her knocking her into the hedge and worse, ripping her nylons.

His sins kept piling up until the day a teacher from high school pulled into our driveway for a visit, and Buckwheat jumped into his car to greet him. It was love for them both. On the teacher's next visit we insisted they should stay together and cheered when they left. That dog did not even look back! When we heard the following year that the teacher and his wife divorced we were sure we knew the reason why! She probably issued an ultimatum: "Me or that dog." And Buckwheat stayed with a smile. The last I heard man and dog were still together after many years.

Changing with Time

Although we were only a few miles from the town where I'd spent most of my life, I was aware of the changing seasons as I had never been before. When we lived in town going out meant driving on errands single-mindedly and returning home, perhaps not even noticing the weather. Winter meant I turned on the heater. Summer the kids were out of school.

Now that I saw nature all the time, I spent most of my days outdoors and plainly noticed the changing seasons. The glorious Technicolor blossoms in spring; with the milder weather bringing out birds we missed all winter; new babies of every breed repopulated our landscape changing the cold, grey days into a scene that rivaled a Disney movie. Green shoots appeared overnight changing the gold hills to emerald.

Rain or shine, the animals needed care, so I donned boots and jacket and went to work. Being outdoors made me aware of the differences. There was misty rain that hung like a fine veil and allowed the animals to continue their everyday quest for food and adventure. Then there was the heavy, pounding, intermittent rain that had us all seeking temporary shelter.

Summer, with its welcome natural warmth, gave us time to replenish our stock of wood. I remember the vast blue bowl of sky with hawks catching air currents and drawing circles, the sprinkler producing sparkling rainbows while we ran through it to cool off, and, of course, watching our various ducks bobbing in the pond, flapping their wings in obvious joy.

Large acres on the south side of the house produced golden grasses that gently swayed in the breeze, mimicking ocean waves. Once it was about waist-high large machines arrived to cut it down and bale these tender golden shoots which would appear again in the spring.

Autumn rained down leaves, each as different as snowflakes, giving us a golden and red carpet that stuck to shoes and fur and transferred their glory into the house. The slight chill reminded us of what was just around the corner. Yes, winter, but also the propane man.

Bundling up with our breath a grey fog in front of us, looking at a thick grey blanket over the once blue sky, the bare trees with skeleton arms, we are nevertheless outside doing what has to be done every day. It is heartening to see the animals don't seem to mind the weather; it's another fine day to them, reminding us that every day is a great day for us, too. I do, however, check closely for signs of early spring. I really don't like winter.

Douglas, a friend, Buckwheat, Chuck and David

Memories Remain

As with everything in life there are beginnings and endings and our adventures were coming to an end. We were only renting paradise after all, and now it was unfortunately being sold. It was becoming harder to live far away from transportation with children growing up—some leaving school, some going off to start new lives, so it was a with a mixture of sadness and expectation that we began hunting for a house to buy so we could remain in this beautiful little town.

We gathered together little mementos—goose eggs, blue green eggs all with contents blown out; bouquets of feathers—gold, striped, red—from almost every breed of fowl that had shared space with us; antique bottles from the junk pile; and rat-bitten decorations from the basement.

Best of all, we collected memories. Each of us has our own collection that we happily share with others, brushing off the shiny ones and laying aside some of the more rusty ones. Along with collecting, we had to learn to let go.

We first sold the ponies to people who, like us, were captivated by their beautiful colors and smallness. Maybe they could carry the dream further and hitch them to buggies for small children to enjoy. Next came the cows who found a happy home outside of Vallejo where there was plenty room for them and some of the ducks too.

I think I felt the worst watching the goats leave. A few people answered my ad with the idea of barbequed goat and were surprised when I was horrified at the idea. I would sooner consider eating my dogs! I did place them in good homes with people as eccentric and goat-loving as myself. The picture I will always carry in my head is of a middle-aged lady in an old truck driving down my lane with a goat sitting in the seat beside her. Goosy went to the owner of our place, who promised she would live her life out in peace at his other farm. Rabbits went by the dozen as pets and soon all that remained were dogs, cats and chickens which all came along with us to our new home which had a double lot and felt like country though only blocks from Main Street.

Our moving day was on Thanksgiving. We all gave thanks for everything we had, which was more than most people ever had; ate our store-bought turkey dinner, smelled smoke and rushed out to hose the roof one last time. In the confusion the sweet potatoes were left forgotten in the oven until the next day. One last laugh.

When we all get together, now years later, we share our funny, sad and exciting stories and relive it all over again.

One of my favorite stories took place while we were watching television one evening, and I heard knocking at the picture window. There was a full-grown goat butting his horns against the window, letting us know we had forgotten to put him the barn!

I have been questioned many times about how I could take a vacation with so many animals to care for. My answer was always the same. "Where would I want to go? We used to go camping, but now I am camping in my own park every day. We are in Eden, why would we leave?"

How fortunate we were to have lived in the country, becoming acquainted with all forms of animals and challenges, to experience the serenity that was common then, but is so scarce now. I can truly look back and say we never let fear or good sense deter us from living every day to its fullest and fulfilling our country living dream.

Douglas & David with guns. Chuck with bongos

About the Author

S. Lee Schauer now resides less than twenty-five miles from where her country adventure took place. Her children all live close by as if the farm still exerts its magic pull drawing them near. She has never returned to country living since her nursing career took over much of her time. Now retired, she spends her spare time writing. Her first book, *As I Remember It: the Memoirs of an Old County Nurse* can be found on Amazon.

She and her children remain close, using any excuse for a family get together where they often reminisce over their farm adventures.

The Schauer Family then...

And now
Chuck, Douglas, Me, Terri, and David